T0195962

A through Z
for You and Me!

A Book for Two

This book will make memorizing the alphabet letter names and sounds fun.
Teacher and child may play and read the book, as can child to child or parent to child.

Karen Hutton

This book is a work of non-fiction. Unless otherwise noted, the author and the publisher make no explicit guarantees as to the accuracy of the information contained in this book and in some cases, names of people and places have been altered to protect their privacy.

Archway Publishing books may be ordered through booksellers or by contacting:

Archway Publishing
1663 Liberty Drive
Bloomington, IN 47403
www.archwaypublishing.com
844-669-3957

Because of the dynamic nature of the Internet, any web addresses or links contained in this book may have changed since publication and may no longer be valid. The views expressed in this work are solely those of the author and do not necessarily reflect the views of the publisher, and the publisher hereby disclaims any responsibility for them.

Any people depicted in stock imagery provided by Getty Images are models, and such images are being used for illustrative purposes only.
Certain stock imagery © Getty Images.

Interior Image Credit: Karen Hutton

ISBN: 978-1-4808-9860-8 (sc)
ISBN: 978-1-4808-9861-5 (e)

Print information available on the last page.

Archway Publishing rev. date: 11/09/2020

Dedication

I greatly thank all of my doctors who have cared for me following my 2018 diagnosis of cancer.

I thank my entire family for their love and caring support both in the writing of this book and during my many treatments.

I appreciate the unending support of Marcia K. Horn, JD Director, Exon 20 Group ICAN®, International Cancer Advocacy Network (https://askican.org).

The wonderful team of loving teachers at ACPS Alexandria City Public Schools will always hold a special place in my heart.

My principal Rachael Dischner has always been a strong supporter and without her I never could have survived in kindergarten.

My darling husband and four children have all contributed to my success and survival.

My two dear sisters, Margaret and Helen, have been a continuing source of strength and I'm thankful to them.

The book is dedicated to Helen. She always enjoyed reading and it came easy to her. I never enjoyed it and since then I'm still struggling with the words.

The secret of this book is what has aided me most - repetition, repetition, repetition.

How the book works

The purpose of the book is to provide a resource for children in the Pre-K and Kindergarten classroom.

The book is a super resource for catching up quickly and for children that need the constant repetition in order to learn.

It's a resource for special ed teachers and English as a second language learners. It is a teacher resource book meant to be read with the child.

First, practice and then read teacher to student and then student to student when appropriate.

The teacher says the image name, the letter name and then the letter sound. The sound is repeated several times in order to be said in unison for the comfort and practice of the child.

As kindergarten teachers we did not have an in-class resource for our children. We need to speak to the children and repeat the letter. Many children are dual language learners, so they are already behind the learning curve when they arrive in class. With this book, children will have fun learning the alphabet.

Instructions

First touch and say the letter's name, then say the sound when you go around.

Have some fun and then you are done!

Touch the circled capital letter and say its name. Look at the picture to determine the sound to make, such as A is for Apple.

Say the letter, followed by the sound of the letter, and then described the picture. Start at the letter left of center. Touch the letter and say its sound.

Each capital letter needs the appropriate sound of the picture to be said next to the letter. The letter is first named and then the sound of the letter is said as you go around the circle. When you finish the circle, direct the child to turn the page.

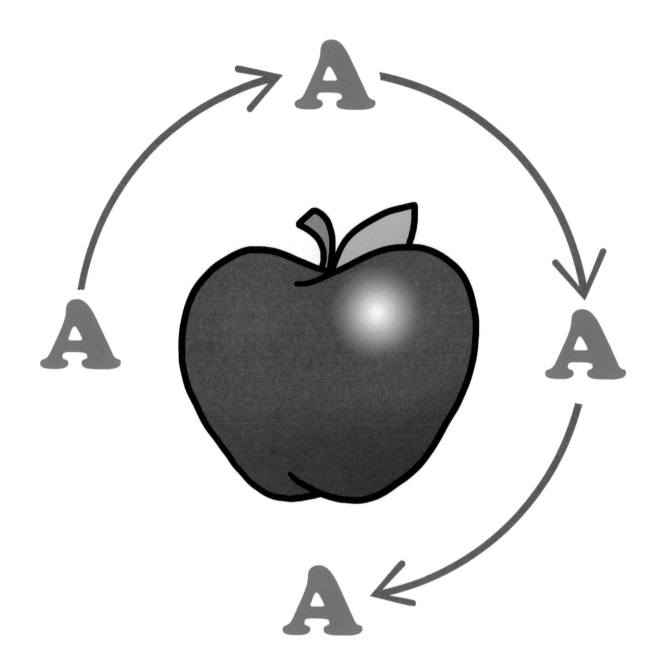

Turn

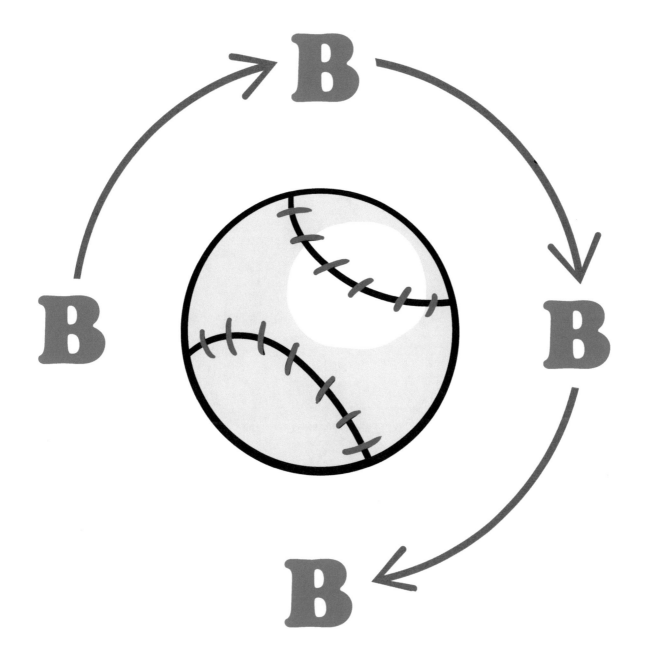

Turn

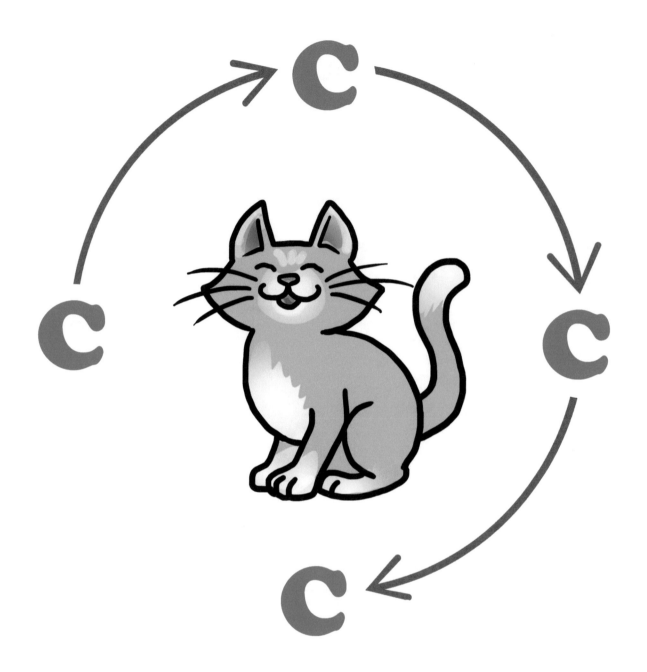

C

C

C

C

C

Turn

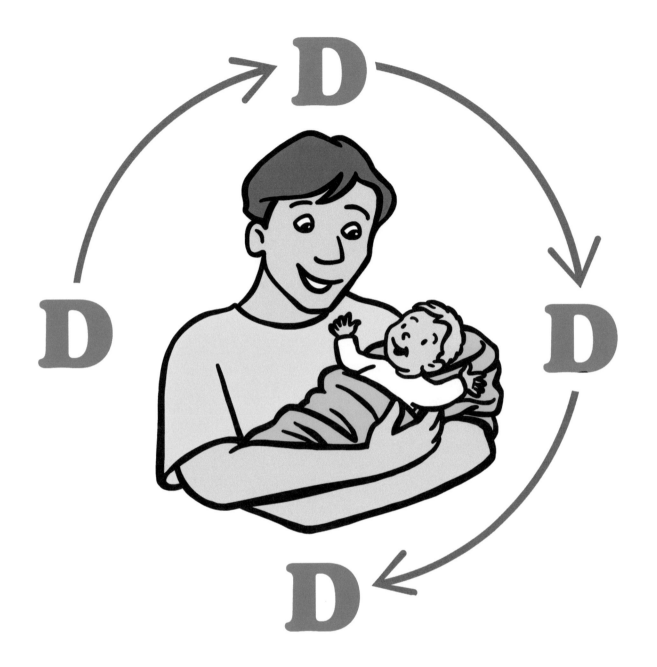

D D D D

D Turn

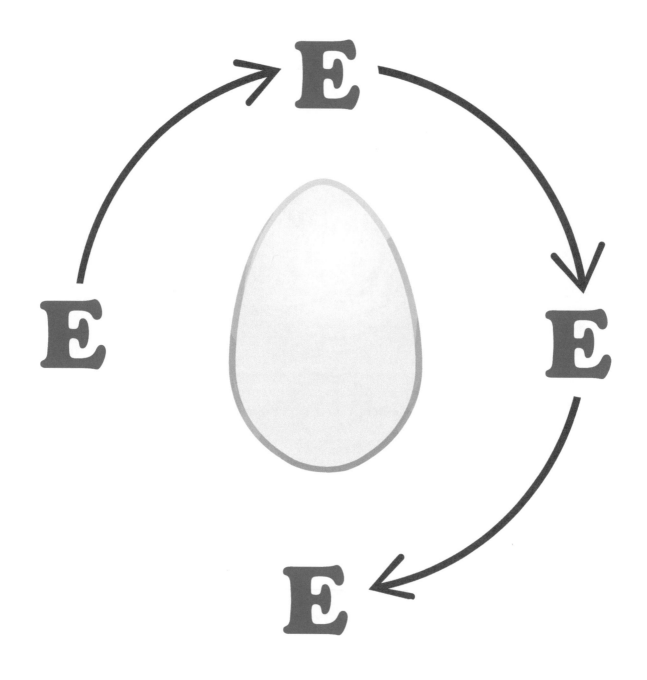

Turn

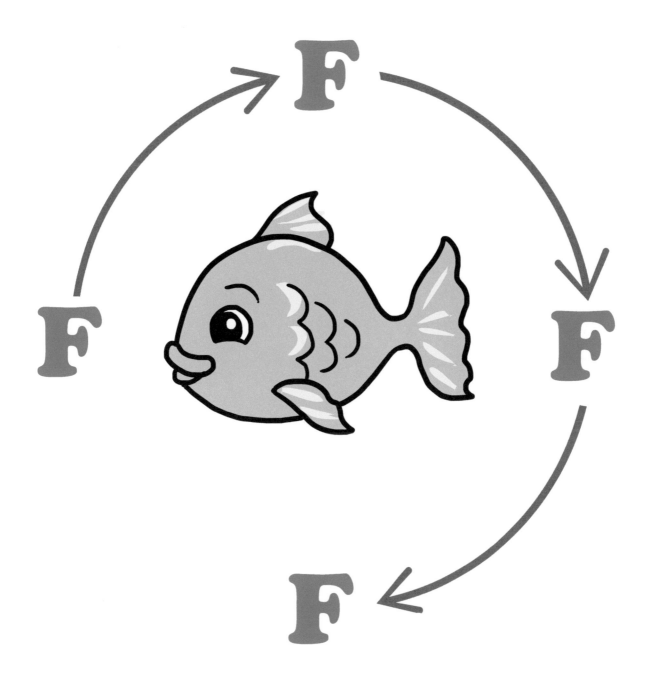

F

Turn

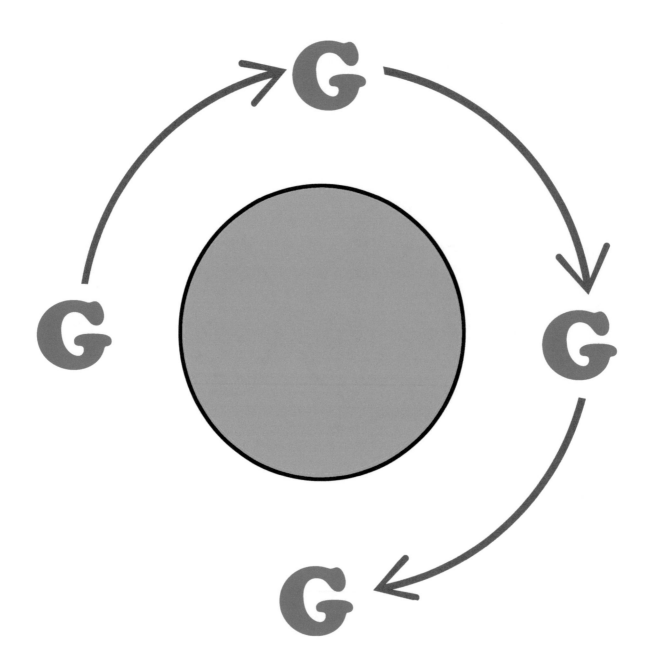

Turn

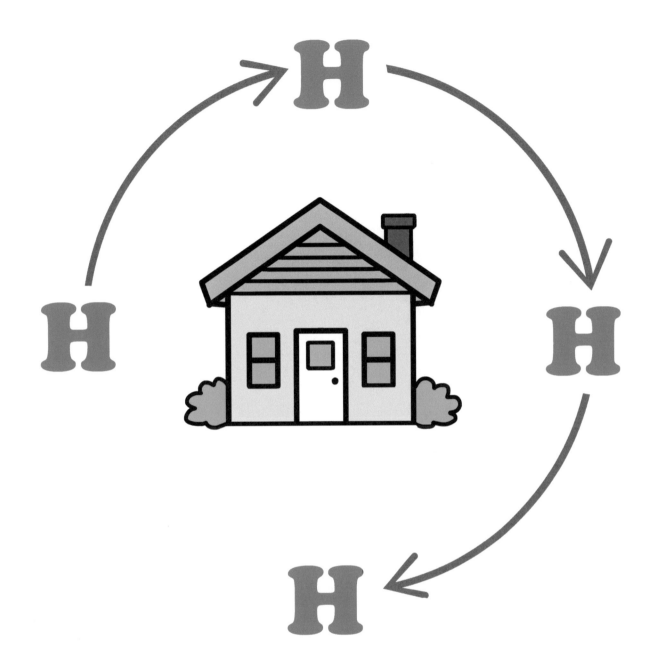

H

Turn

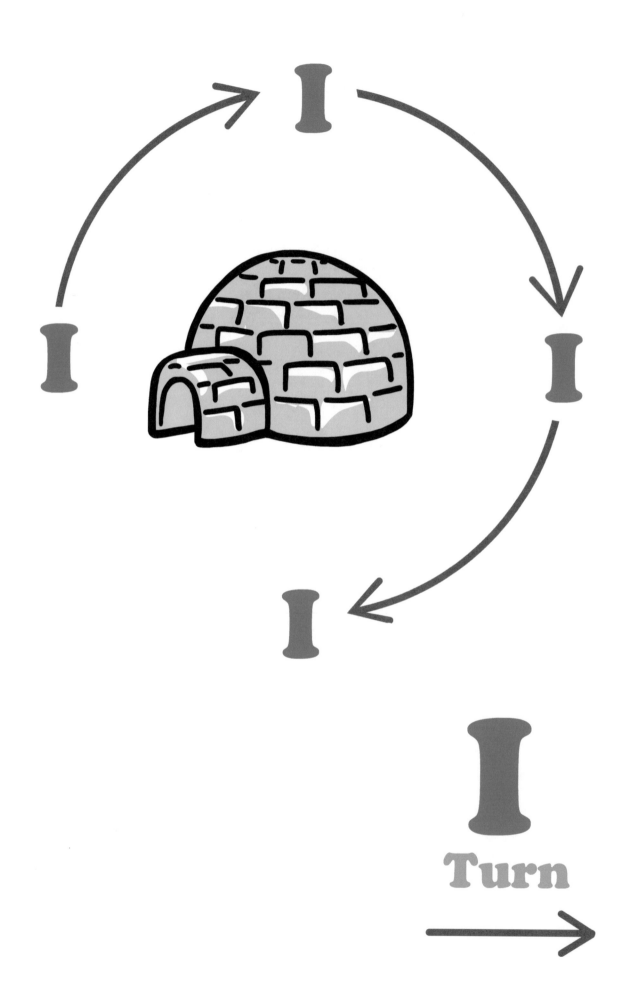

Turn

J

J

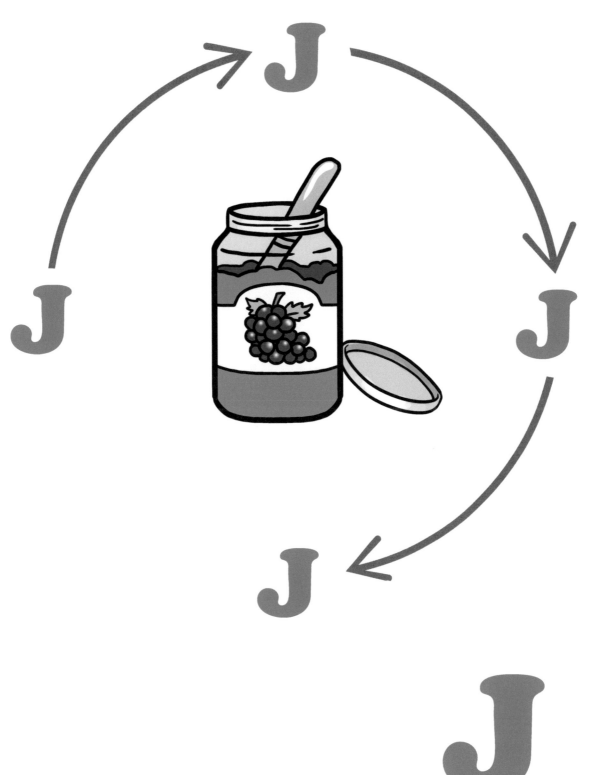

J

J

J

Turn

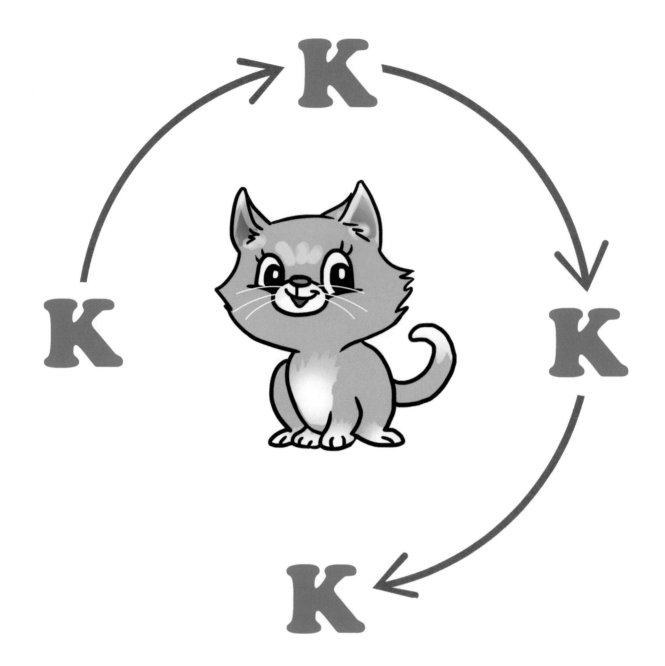

Turn

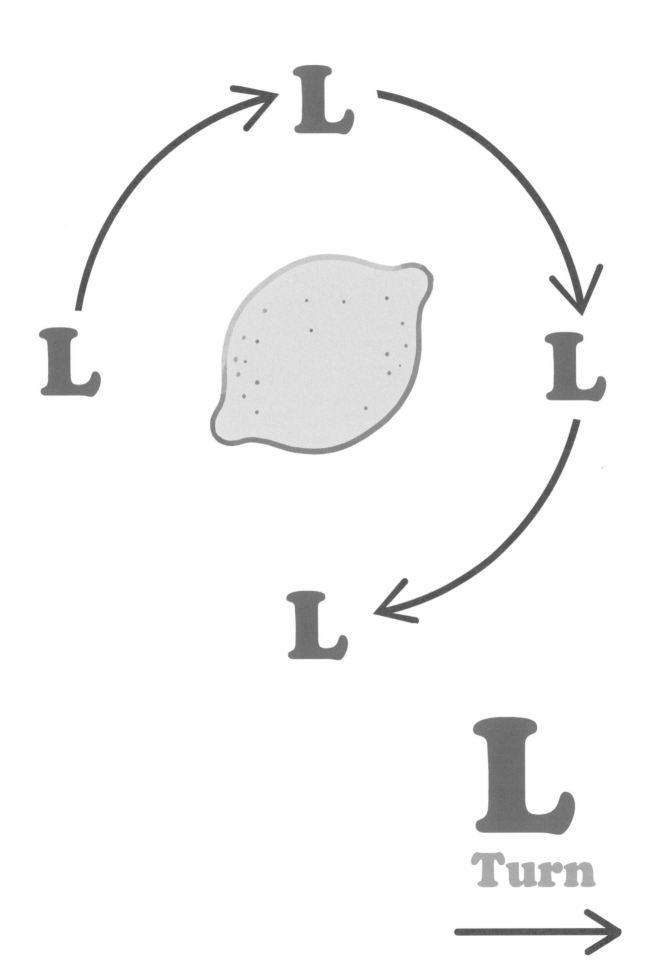

Turn

M
M
M
M

M
Turn

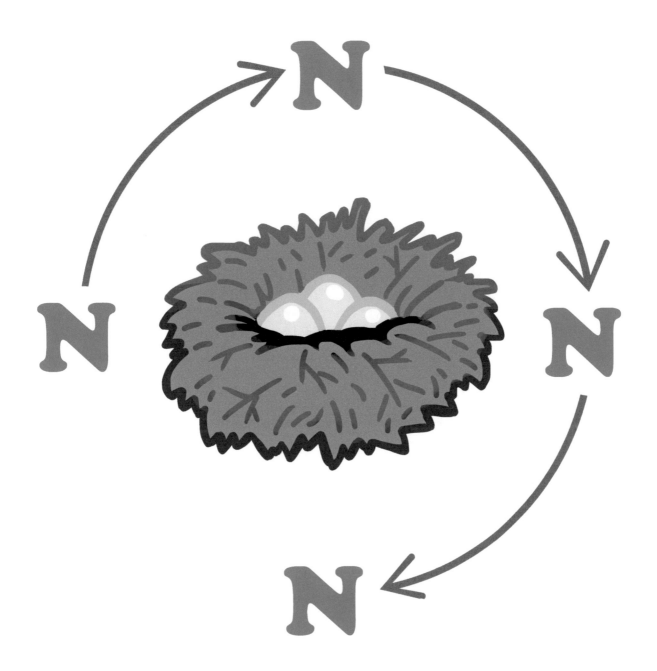

N N N N

N
Turn

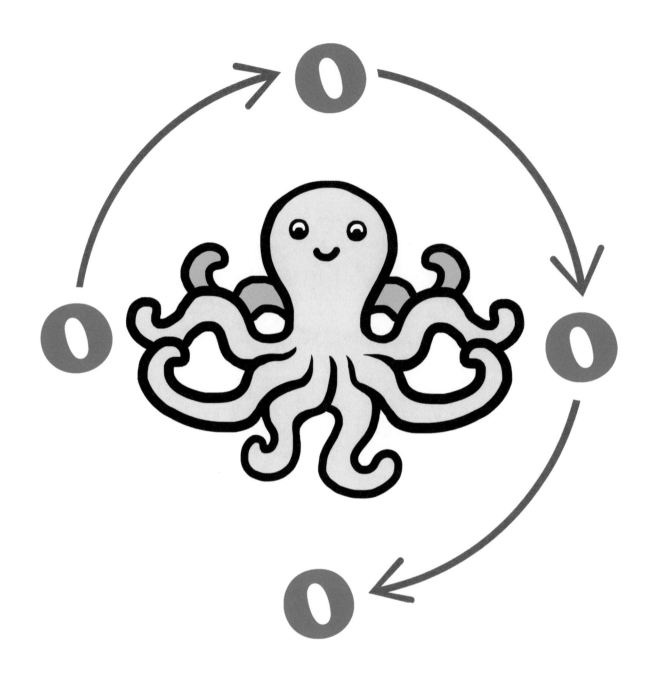

O O O O

Turn

P

P

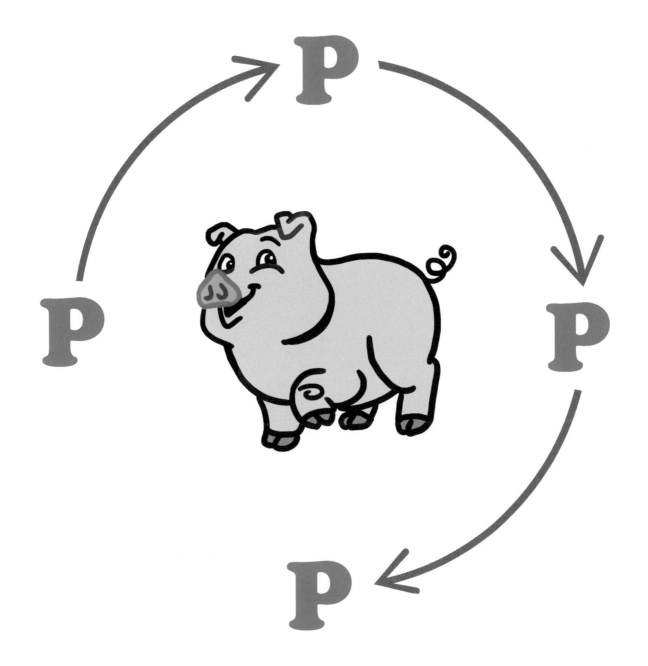

P

P

P

Turn

Turn

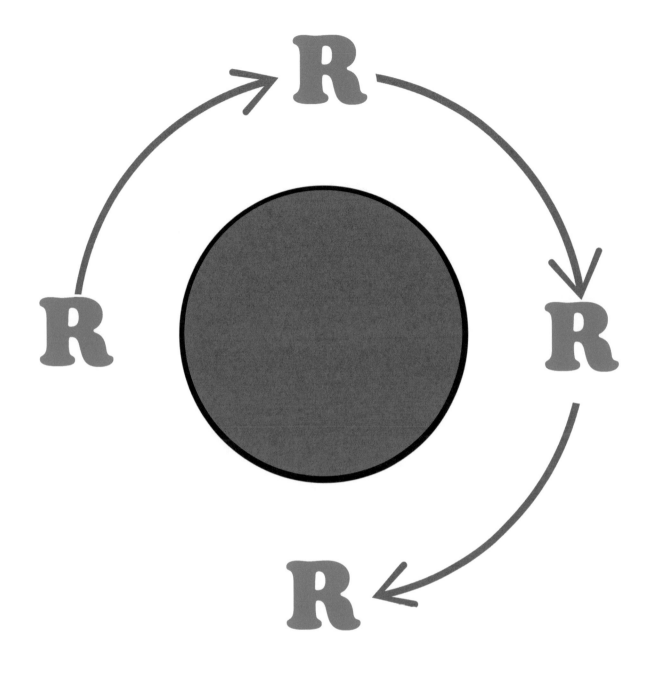

Turn

S S

S

S

Turn

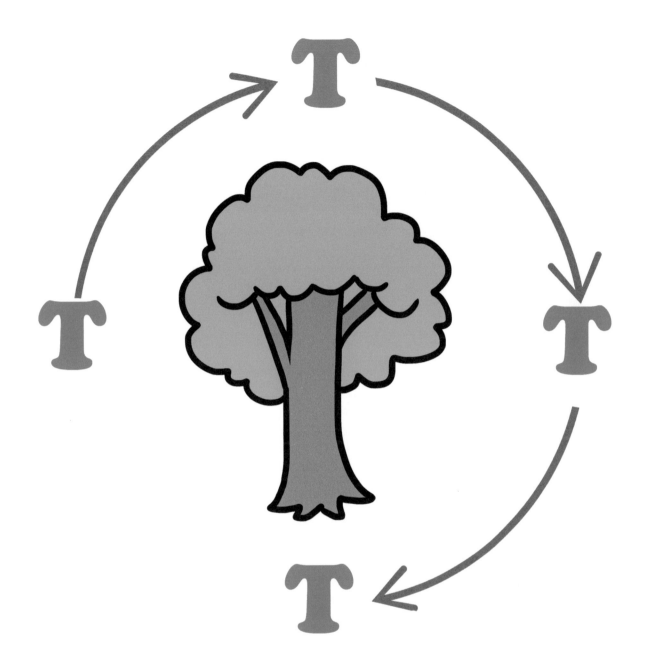

T

Turn

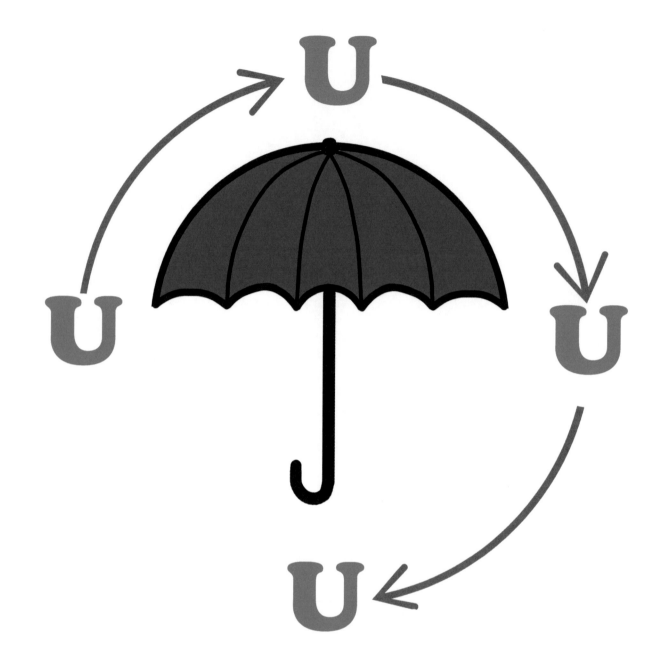

U
U
U
U

U
Turn

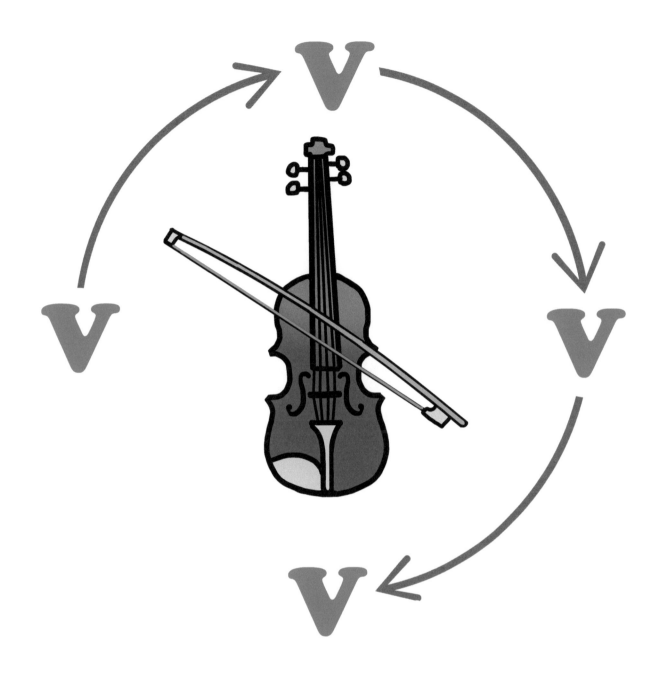

Turn

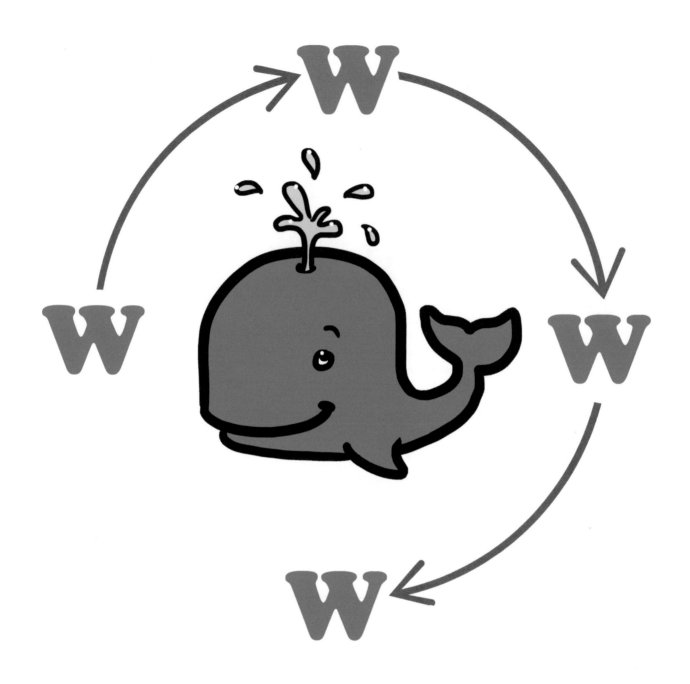

W
W
W
W

W
Turn

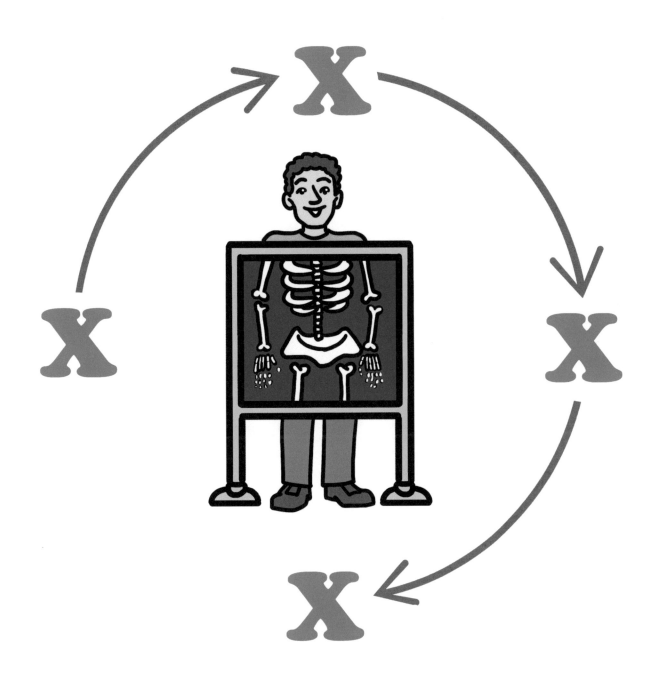

Turn

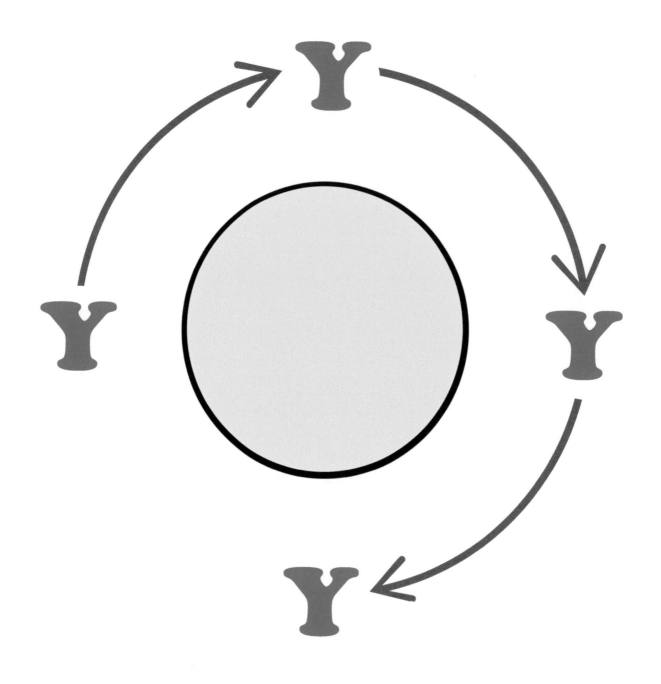

Turn

Z Z Z Z

Z

Turn

The End

About the Author

Karen Hutton is a former Pre-K and Kindergarten teacher is a former kindergarten teacher who seeks to help young children become literate in a fun and positive way.

She and her husband, James, have four children.

She was undergoing whole brain radiation when the inspiration for this book came to me. It is actually an interesting story. She had a strange reaction to the cancer treatments of whole brain radiation and follow-on chemo-therap. She wrote the first draft of this book with her left-hand despite being right-handed.

She worked in kindergarten for years and her desire was driven to write this book to help children.

It just came out of her brain and onto the paper.

Printed in the United States
By Bookmasters